TOCCATA AND FUGUE IN D MINOR

AND OTHER GREAT MASTERPIECES BY BACH, TCHAIKOVSKY, WAGNER AND OTHERS

TRANSCRIBED FOR PIANO

INTRODUCED AND EDITED BY
DANIEL GLOVER

DOVER PUBLICATIONS, INC.
MINEOLA, NEW YORK

Bibliographical Note

This Dover edition, first published in 2014, is a new compilation of works, previously published separately. Bibliographical information for each work can be found on the individual title pages. Daniel Glover has prepared a new Introduction specially for this Dover edition.

International Standard Book Number
ISBN-13: 978-0-486-49298-8
ISBN-10: 0-486-49298-2

Manufactured in the United States by Courier Corporation
49298201   2014
www.doverpublications.com

CONTENTS

Introduction

The piano is an instrument which is ideally suited to playing transcriptions of music from other genres. With merely ten fingers a single person can reproduce the sounds of an orchestra, a singer, a violin, or even an entire operatic cast of solo singers, chorus, plus orchestra. Nearly every pianist wrote their own transcriptions, until the practice eventually fell out of fashion in the later twentieth century. This Dover edition includes a varied assortment of pieces as transcribed by famous pianists, some of whom are remembered today solely for these arrangements. The pieces have been selected with the goal of offering pianists at every level of development the chance to play familiar masterworks on the piano.

A true cosmopolitan, **Eugen d'Albert** (1864–1932) was born in Scotland, of an English mother and a German-born father of French and Italian heritage. D'Albert spent portions of his life in Austria and Germany, where he met Brahms and studied with Liszt, and in 1914 he became a Swiss citizen. A prolific composer of twenty-one operas, two piano concertos, a cello concerto, numerous orchestral, chamber, vocal, and solo piano works, his marriage to the Venezuelan pianist Teresa Carreño (the second of his six wives) spawned a humorous review in a Berlin newspaper: "Yesterday Ms. Carreño played for the first time the Second Concerto of her third husband in the fourth Philharmonic concert."

A passacaglia is an ostinato form, wherein a bass line is repeated throughout with continuously changing accompaniment and contrapuntal variation occurring like tapestry above and around it. Johann Sebastian Bach's **Passacaglia in C minor,** originally for pedal harpsichord and later for organ, begins with an eight bar theme in triple meter, followed by twenty variations and a double fugue. It is the most celebrated work in this form. D'Albert's transcription is faithful to the original and ingeniously incorporates the pedal part into the left hand, sometimes creating the effect of three hands.

Ferruccio Busoni (1866–1924) was one of the most influential, as well as enigmatic, personalities of the late nineteenth and early twentieth centuries. His tremendous technical skills as a pianist dazzled the entire world, but as a composer some felt he lacked inspiration. Busoni was a fervent lifelong advocate for the music of Bach, Mozart, and Liszt. His piano transcriptions of music by Bach were once staples of every pianist's repertoire in the early twentieth century; especially notable are those of the organ chorale preludes and *Chaconne in D minor* for solo violin. His ubiquitous contributions to the transcription genre prompted someone to introduce him at a party as "Mr. Bach-Busoni." Busoni was a master of pedaling and he sometimes used all three pedals at the same time.

"Turandots Frauengemach" (Turandot's Boudoir) is the fourth piece in a set of piano pieces Busoni called *Elegies.* Tracing the germination of this piece is fascinating: an English folk melody ("Greensleeves"), which Busoni mistakenly thought to be a Chinese folksong, was incorporated into his symphonic suite, *Turandot,* then subsumed into an opera of the same name based on the Chinese princess, and finally transcribed as an elegy for solo piano. Busoni's pianistic effects include a double glissando in thirds, and the usage of Liszt's enterprising scale fingerings in which the thumb passes under the fifth finger (see Liszt's *Spanish Rhapsody*).

Alfred Cortot (1877–1962) was a tireless conductor, concert pianist, and teacher whose influence is still felt today. His legacy also includes many fine editions of great works by Liszt, Chopin, Schumann, and others. Cortot was a true poet of the piano and is widely remembered as one of the greatest interpreters of Chopin's music. He was also an enthusiastic supporter of contemporary French composers and wrote an important book on his compatriots and their music.

Cortot's sumptuous transcription of Johannes Brahms' **Wiegenlied (Lullaby), Op. 49, No. 4,** is a tribute to his sensitivity as a pianist. It displays an acute sense of understanding of the various registers of the instrument and gives the pianist an opportunity to project different "voices" as the simple melody moves around the keyboard, each time clothed in different garb.

Sergei Rachmaninoff once said of **Leopold Godowsky** (1870–1938): "[He] is the only musician of this age who has given a real, lasting contribution to the development of the piano." He must have been referencing the technical side of piano writing, rather than any specific compositional approach, for Godowsky's lasting legacy rests largely on his transcriptions for piano, rather than his original compositions. An inveterate transcriber, Godowsky left dozens of solo piano transcriptions from Baroque music, including solo violin and cello works of Bach, to the 53 etudes based on Chopin's Etudes. The tremendous polyphonic complexity and difficulty of many of his works keeps them out of the hands of all but the top virtuoso pianists, and yet Godowsky also left some delightful miniatures that display his genius.

Two of Godowsky's more approachable transcriptions are the familiar **Tango** by Albéniz and Brahms' **Wiegenlied (Lullaby).** In the case of the Albéniz transcription, Godowsky has breathed new life into a familiar classic by adding some tasteful decorations that don't detract from the original melody, but enliven it. The addition of some chromatic modifications of the harmony is a hallmark of Godowsky's style. It cannot be stressed enough how important and instructive it is to study Godowsky's fingerings. The Brahms *Wiegenlied* transcription is a fine example of this, for there is virtually no note which doesn't have a fingering written on it. This arrangement was evidently written for pianists of moderate skill for pedagogical purposes.

Australian pianist **Percy Grainger** (1882–1961) was a staunch proponent of new music, as well as an avid collector of folksongs. His fame now rests on such lightweight pieces as the folksong arrangements *Country Gardens* and *Molly on the Shore*. His catalogue of transcriptions includes not only the many folksong settings from America, Britain, Denmark, and even the Faroe Islands, but there are also many transcriptions of opera, ballet, orchestral, and vocal music.

Grainger's setting of Brahms' **Wiegenlied (Lullaby)** is more elaborate than those by Cortot and Godowsky. Grainger's meticulous markings should be followed throughout. Notice the extensive use of the sostenuto (middle) pedal. He thanked his teacher, Busoni, for introducing him to this often overlooked feature of the modern piano.

Another beautiful transcription is that of the **Irish Tune from County Derry,** which is included in his collection of British folksong arrangements. The tune is generally known as "Londonderry Air," but also goes by the familiar title "Danny Boy" when a different set of lyrics is applied to the same melody.

Peter Ilyitch Tchaikovsky's perennial favorite ballet, *The Nutcracker,* is here represented by Grainger's disarmingly effective **Paraphrase on the Waltz of the Flowers.** Liszt's influence is in evidence throughout the piece, remarkably written when Grainger was in his early twenties. Virtuoso alternating octaves cleverly imitate the harp cadenza which opens the waltz. Of special interest is the modern harmony that at times appears to predict future developments in jazz.

Theodor Leschetizky (1830–1915) was perhaps the most influential piano teacher in the entire Romantic period. This selective list of his pupils includes some of the most outstanding piano virtuosos of all time: Ignacy Paderewski, Artur Schnabel, Paul Wittgenstein, Ignaz Friedman, Alexander Brailowsky and Benno Moiseiwitsch. If there was a "Leschetizky Method" it certainly was his ability to bring out the very best from each individual pupil. Liszt and Leschetizky both studied with Beethoven's pupil Carl Czerny, and many current day pianists can trace the lineage of their teachers directly back to Beethoven through either Liszt or Leschetizky.

Although Leschetizky composed over one hundred character pieces for the piano, a piano concerto, two operas, as well as an assortment of songs, his music is sadly forgotten today. There are a handful of transcriptions that have kept his name alive as a composer. Leschetizky's version of Franz Schubert's **Moment Musical in F minor, Op. 94, No. 3** should be compared with Schubert's original score, because it is more detailed in its tonal aspects, particularly regarding dynamics and use of various registers. It should be noted that the original title of Schubert's piece was "Russian Air," and that Leschetizky instructs the pianist to play it in a "Hungarian manner!"

Among the illustrious ranks of Polish born virtuoso pianists, including Godowsky, Leschetizky, Schulz-Evler, and Tausig, is **Moritz Moszkowski** (1854–1925). Moszkowski was the ultimate salon composer, having contributed a plethora of short, brilliant, but exceedingly well crafted lightweight original compositions for the piano, in addition to many incomparable transcriptions. Moszkowski's self-effacing attitude is no more humorously displayed than in his response to a request for his autobiography: "I should be happy to send you my piano concerto but for two reasons: first, it is worthless; second, it is most convenient (the score being 400 pages long) for making my piano stool higher when I am engaged in studying better works."

Moszkowski's sparkling virtuoso transcription of themes from Georges Bizet's *Carmen*, titled **Chanson**

Bohême, begins with a reference to the "Sequidilla" from Act I, and then segues directly into the "Gypsy Song," which opens Act II. The dazzling piano writing includes double thirds, rapid repeated notes, and scintillating alternating hand chord technique which amply displays Moszkowski's phenomenal prowess as a pianist.

Written for *The Etude Magazine* in 1919, Moszkowski's transcription of George Frideric Handel's aria **"Lascia ch'io pianga"** from *Rinaldo* is simple and straightforward. The text of the aria is as follows:

> *Let me weep*
> *my cruel fate,*
> *and sigh for liberty.*
> *May sorrow break these chains*
> *Of my sufferings, for pity's sake.*

Among the well-known instrumental excerpts from Felix Mendelssohn's incidental music to *A Midsummer Night's Dream*, Op. 61 is the **"Nocturne"** which accompanies the sleeping lovers and appears between Acts III and IV. Moszkowski's arrangement is so natural on the piano that it almost appears to be a forgotten piece from Mendelssohn's own series of piano pieces known as *Songs Without Words.* As in the Handel transcription, this exquisite arrangement was also apparently composed specially for *The Etude Magazine* in 1920.

Moszkowski's transcription of the **"Barcarolle"** from Jacques Offenbach's *Tales of Hoffmann* begins in a manner similar to that of his *Carmen* transcription. Namely, a theme from a different part of the opera (the duet "C'est une chanson d'amour") opens the work and serves as an introduction to the "Barcarolle." Moszkowski brings back the same unrelated material as a coda; a fine touch of artistic license.

Russian pianist **Anton Rubinstein** (1829–94) was considered by many to be the only serious rival of Franz Liszt. His temperament was tempestuous and his power at the instrument left listeners limp. His physical resemblance to Ludwig van Beethoven added to his mystique, and helped garner respect as an interpreter of the great German composer's music. Liszt called him "Van II." As a composer, Rubinstein left a voluminous catalogue, including over two hundred individual piano pieces spread out over one hundred and twenty published opuses. There were also over a dozen operas, as well as the once popular *"Ocean" Symphony;* and his Piano Concerto No. 4 in D minor was at one time a standard piece in the repertoire. Such popular parlor classics as the *Melody in F,* and *Kamennoi Ostrow* were known by every amateur pianist

a generation ago. Rubinstein's legacy as a musical force continues to this day, because he was the founder of the St. Petersburg Conservatory.

Rubinstein's transcription of Beethoven's beloved **"Turkish March"** from *The Ruins of Athens* is a spirited arrangement full of infectious vigor and requiring the kind of physical strength, as well as a large span, that Rubinstein was known for.

The remarkable lifespan of **Camille Saint-Saëns** (1835–1921) encompassed the entire Romantic era, and extended well into the early twentieth century. It is astounding to imagine that he was born just twelve years after the death of Beethoven, he outlived Debussy, and he was present at the premiere of Stravinsky's *The Rite of Spring.* Conservative by nature, he must have been deeply disturbed to see how far music had come since the Romantic music he had grown up with. This inordinately gifted musical mind was devoted to composing music that pleased and entertained the audience, rather than stirring their emotions.

Saint-Saëns' *Caprice on Airs from Alceste* by Gluck represents a type of free setting of works from the Baroque period, and is one of the most successful examples in the genre. It begins with the grand ballet music from Act II, and then skips forward to a section for the chorus in 3/8 time. In the original opera, Alceste sings a lament in G minor inserted between strains of the chorus. Saint-Saëns follows this structure, but in the spirit of the "da capo aria," provides scintillating piano figuration to embellish the choral theme upon its return. The version included in this volume omits a fugal section of considerable length, which is based on the ballet music. Presumably, this cut was made with the composer's blessing, since it was published in this form during his lifetime.

Adolf Schulz-Evler (1852–1905) was a pupil of fellow Pole, Carl Tausig, and his only lasting contribution to piano literature is his remarkably effective *Concert Arabesques on "By the Beautiful Blue Danube"* by Johann Strauss, Jr. Schulz-Evler left just over fifty solo piano works, including the virtuosic *Variations in G major,* and *Rhapsodie Russe* for piano and orchestra. His name will endure as long as there are daredevil pianists who are willing to tackle the finger crushing challenges of his *Concert Arabesques.* It has been customary for some pianists to omit the opening introduction and begin the transcription at the "Tempo di Valse" indication.

Giovanni Sgambati (1841–1914) was an Italian pianist, with an English mother, who studied with Liszt.

Sgambati was particularly drawn to German composers, especially Beethoven, and he introduced such important works as Beethoven's *"Emperor" Concerto* to Italian audiences in Rome. As with Schulz-Evler, we remember Sgambati today principally for one beloved transcription, that of Christoph Willibald Gluck's **"Melody" from Orfeo ed Euridice.** This melody appears in Act II as the second of three ballet movements and is titled "Dance of the Blessed Spirits." Sgambati's arrangement is written on three staves. The middle staff should be played by the right hand when the stems go up and the left hand when the stems go down.

Born in Warsaw of Jewish parents, **Carl Tausig** (1841–71) was acknowledged by Liszt to be his favorite pupil. Liszt claimed he had never seen such a phenomenon when the boy was presented to him at the age of fourteen. Tausig had an encyclopedic knowledge of the piano repertoire as it then existed and is said to have known most of it by memory. Anton Rubinstein called Tausig "the infallible," due to his reputation of playing with the utmost accuracy, and clarity. His untimely death at the age of twenty-nine robbed the music world of a uniquely gifted performer, as well as prevented him from developing into a mature composer. His scant amount of original compositions includes fewer than a dozen pieces, all for solo piano. The score of his only piano concerto has not survived.

Tausig's transcription of Bach's organ **Toccata and Fugue in D minor** was at one time a virtual requirement to open nearly every piano recital. Tausig reveled in the virtuosic possibilities which are only hinted at in the original organ version. Where the organ plays single notes, Tausig never missed an opportunity to substitute virtuoso octaves. The final Adagio could not have been more grandly presented on the piano, with its sweeping arpeggios.

Schubert composed three *Marches Militaries, D. 733,* for piano four hands. The first of the three, **Marche Militaire No. 1 in D major,** has eclipsed the other two in popularity. Tausig transposed it to the much richer and sonorous key of D-flat major. Comparison with Schubert's original version reveals that Tausig virtually recomposed the piece, to its benefit, as the original version seems like a pale and ineffective simplified version.

Among Tausig's eight transcriptions of music by Wagner are two from *Die Walküre.* **"Siegmund's Love Song"** is from the end of Act I, and Tausig cleverly introduces this excerpt, also known as "Winterstürme," with his own chromatic rumination on a phrase from the middle of the piece. The admirable modulation from C-sharp minor to the home key of B-flat major is worthy of Wagner himself.

Wagner's **Ride of the Valkyries,** from Act III of *Die Walküre,* is perhaps one of the most famous pieces in all of classical music. Even though it is impossible to reproduce the orchestra's volume on one piano, Tausig nonetheless pulls off this feat in an accomplished and masterly manner. For example, the solutions he employed to reproduce the trills as they travel around the orchestra in different registers is nothing short of miraculous. The trills in alternating chords between the two hands produce an intensely visceral excitement.

For its time, Karl Maria von Weber's **Invitation to the Dance** (1819) was an innovative and impressive composition, which he dedicated to his wife. It is said to be the very first concert waltz by any composer (in other words a piece not meant to be danced, but rather performed in concert). It tells the story of a man asking a woman for her consent to dance with him, followed by her consent and the dance itself. The piece concludes with them parting their ways. Tausig's concert arrangement bristles with such virtuoso "tricks" as octave glissandos, blind thirds, double notes, interlocking octaves, and an ear tinkling cadenza in the upper register of the piano, which Tausig added at the beginning of the piece before the actual waltz begins.

DANIEL GLOVER
2014

Toccata and Fugue in D minor

and Other Great Masterpieces by Bach, Tchaikovsky, Wagner and Others

Transcribed for Piano

To Dr. Alexis Kall

Tango

Concert arrangement by Leopold Godowsky

ISAAC ALBÉNIZ

Passacaglia in C minor

Arranged for piano by Eugen d'Albert

JOHANN SEBASTIAN BACH

8

Thema fugatum *(etwas rascher)*

Toccata and Fugue in D minor

Arranged for piano by Carl Tausig

JOHANN SEBASTIAN BACH

D. Appleton and Co., New York, 1923

FUGA
Allegro

Turkish March
from *The Ruins of Athens*

Arranged for piano by Anton Rubinstein

LUDWIG VAN BEETHOVEN

D. Appleton and Co., New York, 1923

Chanson Bohême
from *Carmen*

Arranged for piano by Maurice Moszkowski

GEORGES BIZET

Poco animato.

Wiegenlied
(Lullaby)

Arranged for piano by Alfred Cortot

JOHANNES BRAHMS

Fœtisch Frères S. A., Editeurs, Lausanne.
73, Boulevard Raspail, Paris (VIc)
Copyright by Fœtisch Frères, S. A. 1953.

Wiegenlied
(Lullaby)

Arranged for piano by Leopold Godowsky

JOHANNES BRAHMS

Wiegenlied
(Lullaby)

Arranged for piano by Percy Grainger

JOHANNES BRAHMS

The notes in large type should be played well to the fore
The notes in small type should be played accompanyingly

Schott & Co., London, 1923

Top notes of the melody to the fore.

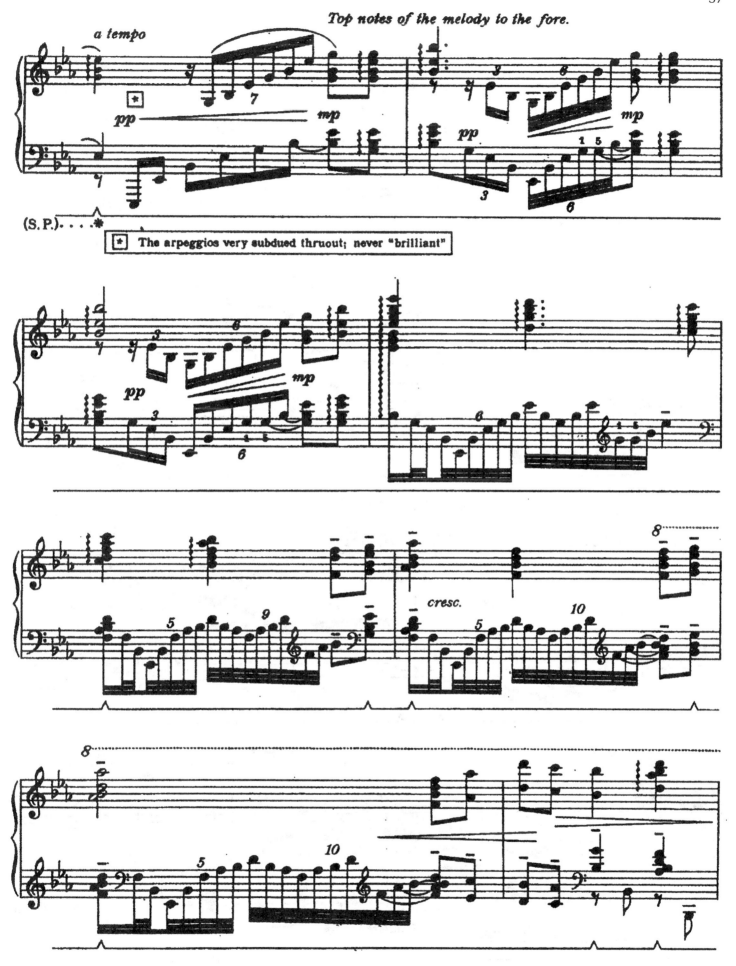

The arpeggios very subdued thruout; never "brilliant"

(Large notes to the fore. Small notes accompanyingly)

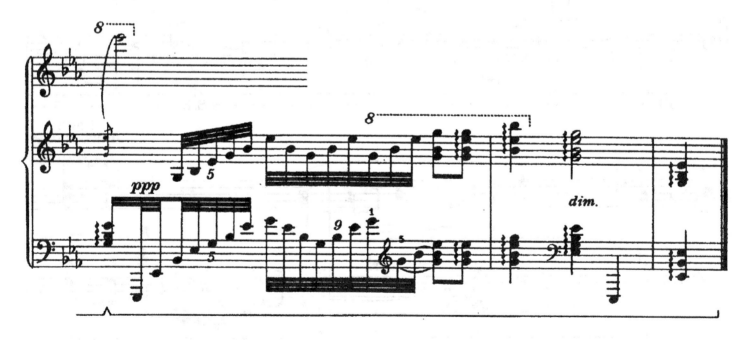

Turandots Boudoir
(Greensleeves)

FERRUCCIO BUSONI

Copyright 1905, by Breitkopf & Härtel, New York.
Aufführungsrecht vorbehalten.

Come da principio.

(quasi Trombe lontanissime)

Melody
from *Orfeo ed Euridice*

Arranged for piano by Giovanni Sgambati

CHRISTOPH WILLIBALD GLUCK

Stich und Druck von B. SCHOTT'S SÖHNE in Mainz.

Fine

Caprice on Airs from Alceste

Arranged for piano by Camille Saint-Saëns   CHRISTOPH WILLIBALD GLUCK

Allegro

D. Appleton & Co., New York, 1923

Lascia ch'io pianga
from *Rinaldo*

Arranged for piano by Maurice Moszkowski

GEORGE FRIDERIC HANDEL

Nocturne
from the music to *Midsummer Night's Dream*

Arranged for piano by Maurice Moszkowski

FELIX MENDELSSOHN

Barcarolle
from *Tales of Hoffmann*

Arranged for piano by Maurice Moszkowski

JACQUES OFFENBACH

Moderato.

Moment Musical in F minor
Op. 94, No. 3 (D. 780)

Concert arrangement by Theodor Leschetizky

FRANZ SCHUBERT

Leipzig: Rahter, 1882

Tempo I.

Marche Militaire
Op. 51, No. 1 (D.733)

Arranged for solo piano by Carl Tausig

FRANZ SCHUBERT

D. Appleton and Co., New York, 1923

Un poco piu tranquillo

Concert Arabesques on
"By the Beautiful Blue Danube"

Arranged for piano by Adolf Schulz-Evler

JOHANN STRAUSS, JR.

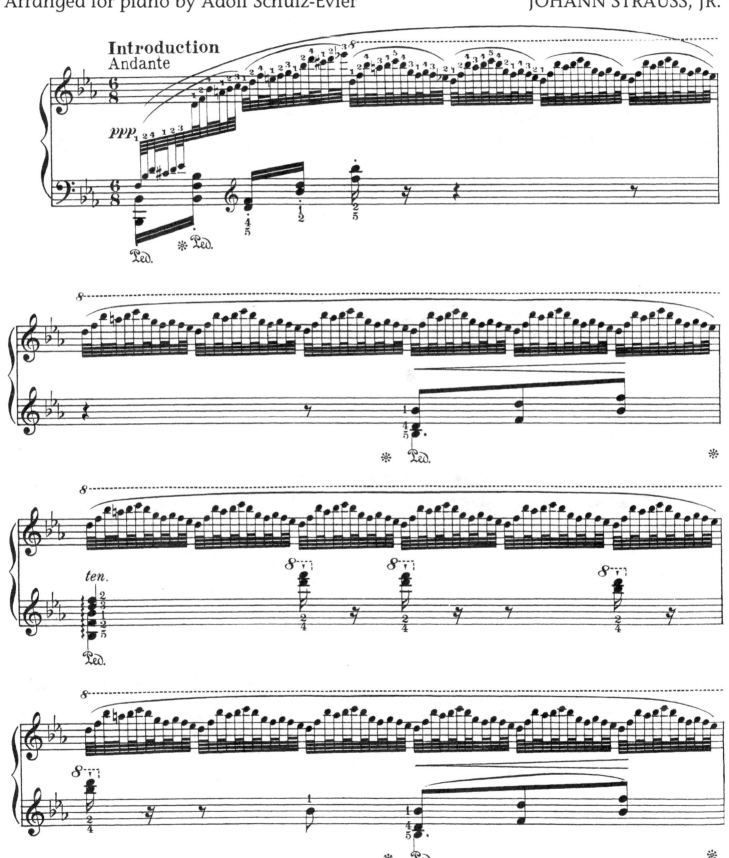

D. Appleton and Co., New York, 1923

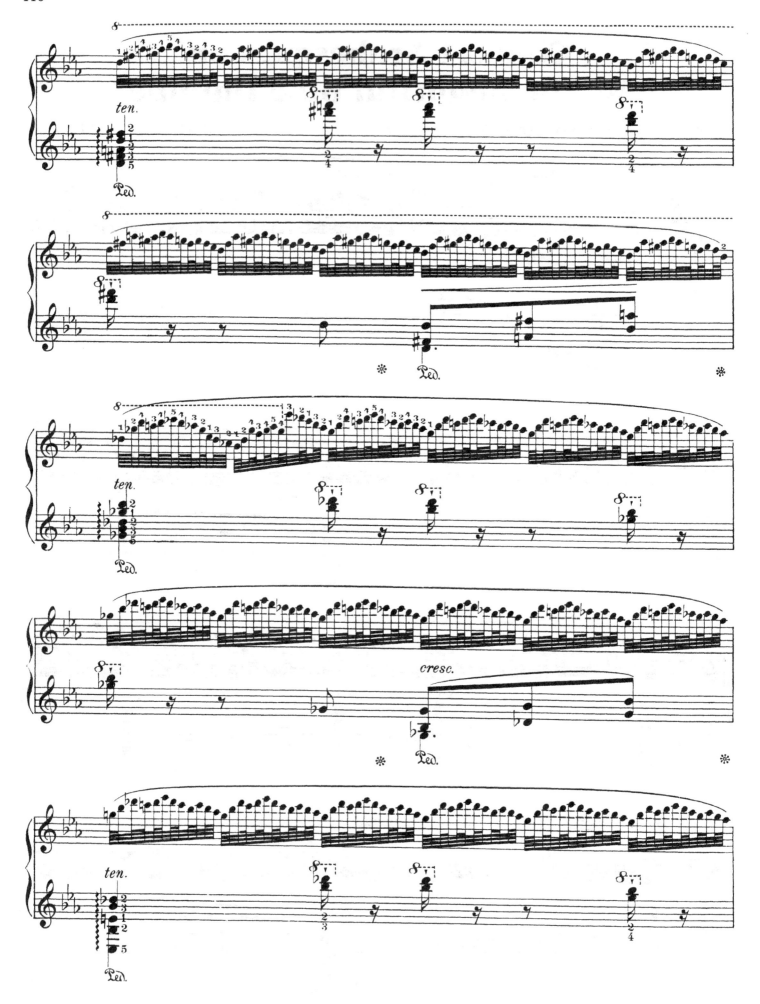

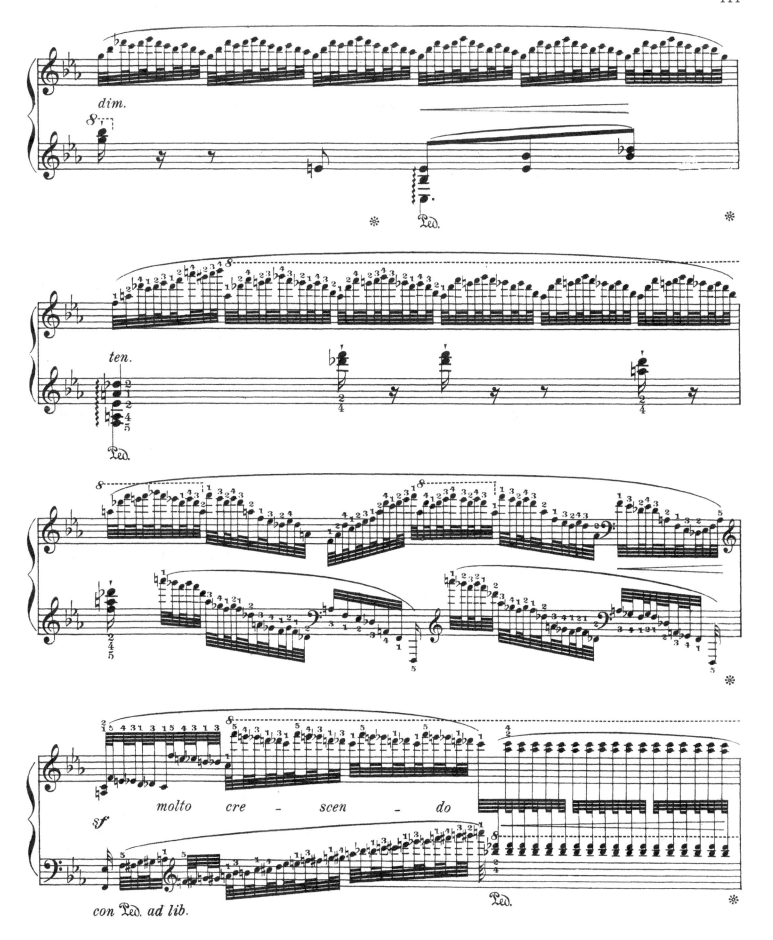

Tempo di Valse

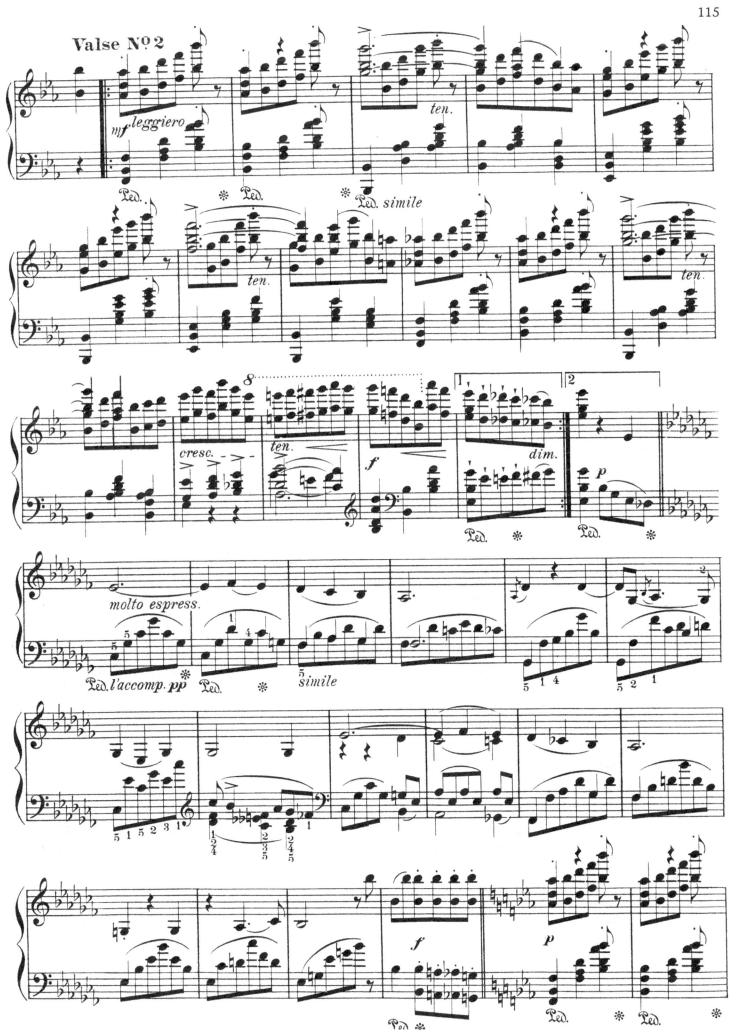

Valse Nº 4

120

Valse № 5 et Coda

124

For Léon Delafosse, in admiration and friendship.

Paraphrase on the Waltz of the Flowers
from *The Nutcracker*

Arranged for piano by Percy Grainger

PETER ILYITCH TCHAIKOVSKY

left hand very mellow

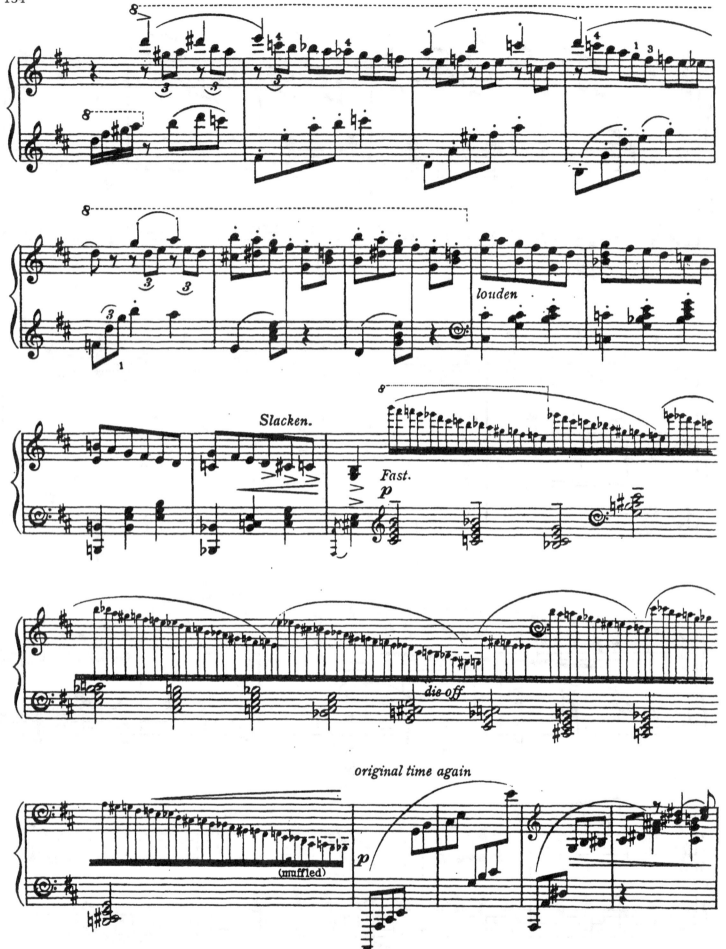

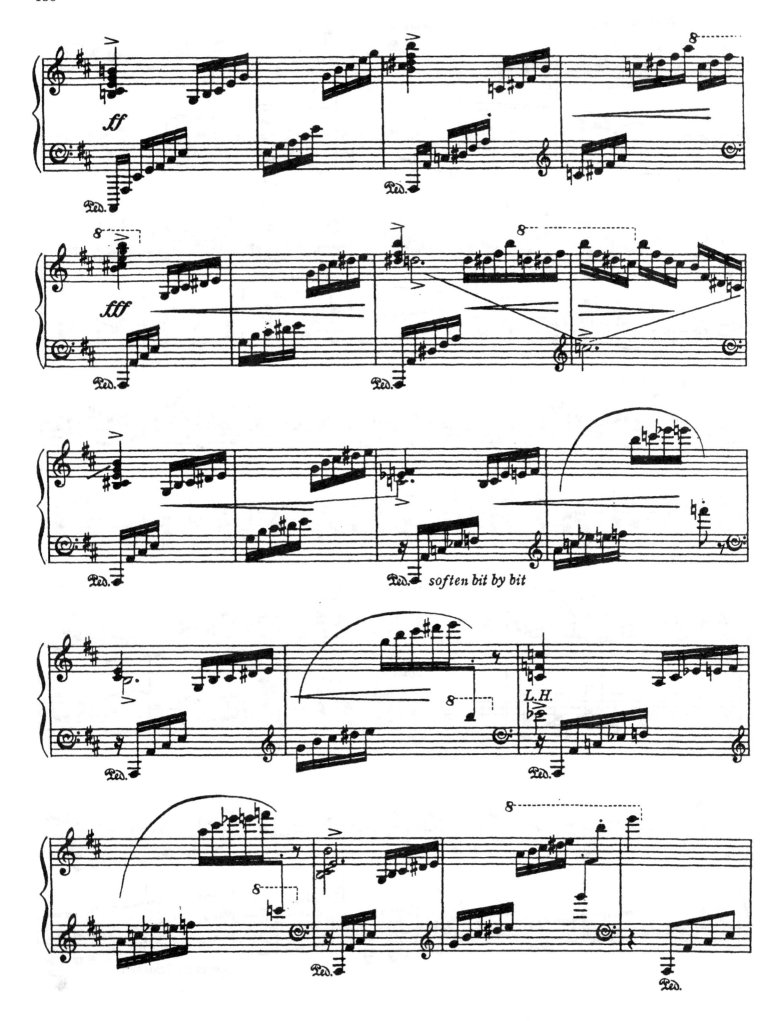

138

Irish Tune from County Derry

Arranged for piano by Percy Grainger

The tune is thro'out printed in bigger notes

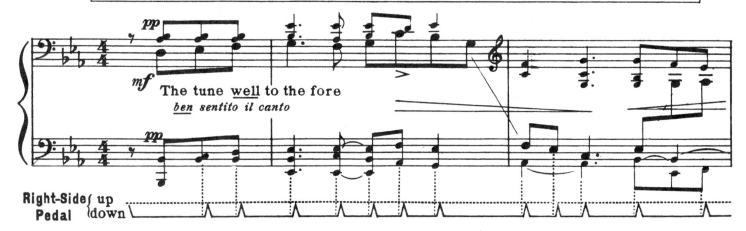

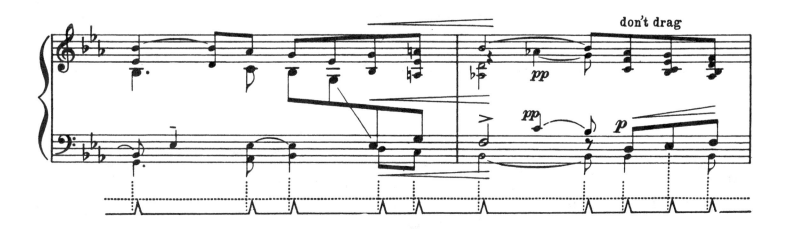

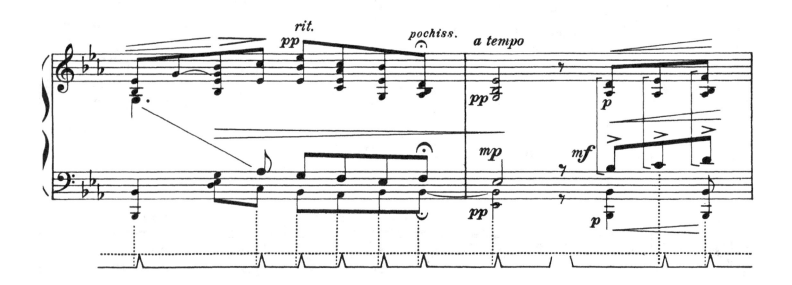

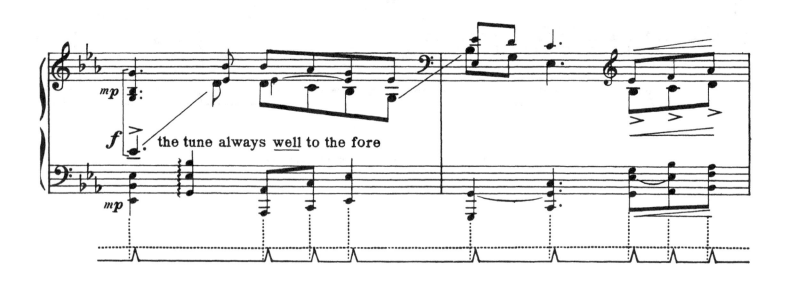

* This note (here altered by me) is B♮ in the original. *P. G.*

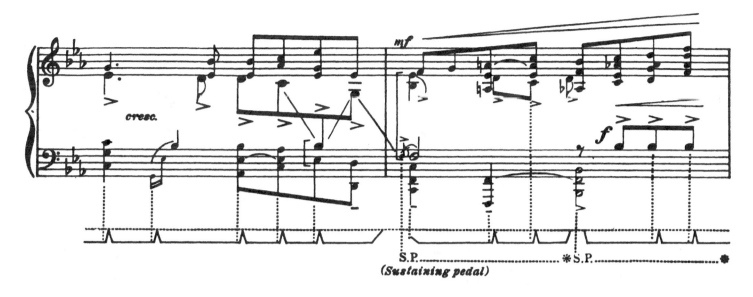

S.P._____
(Sustaining pedal)

S.P._____

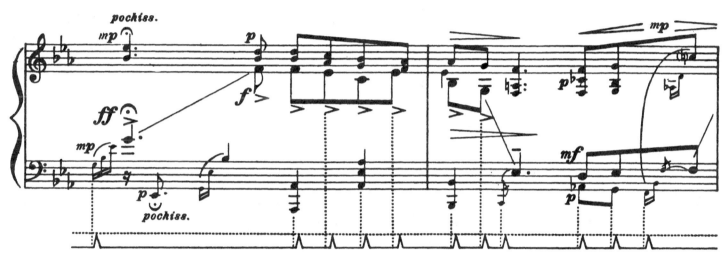

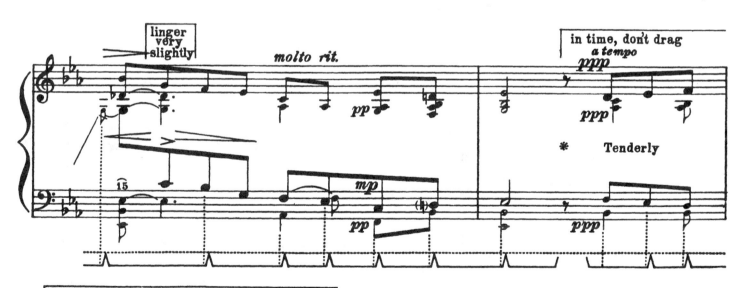

* If you like, the passage between * and ** may be played an octave higher (in both hands)

These middle notes well to the fore:
B A G F E

D G F E D C

don't drag; if anything, slightly faster

* This note (here altered by me) is B♮ in the original. *P. G.*

Ride of the Valkyries
from *Die Walküre*

Arranged for piano by Carl Tausig

RICHARD WAGNER

Mainz: B. Schott's Söhne, n.d.

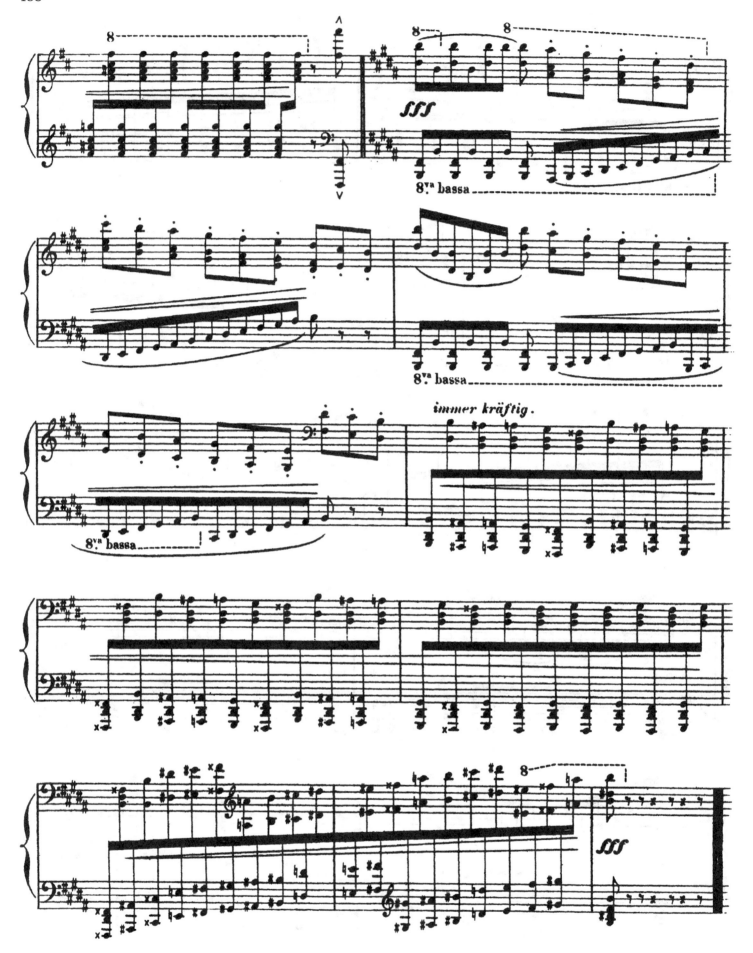

Siegmund's Love Song
from *Die Walküre*

Arranged for piano by Carl Tausig

RICHARD WAGNER

Mainz: B. Schott's Söhne, ca. 1870

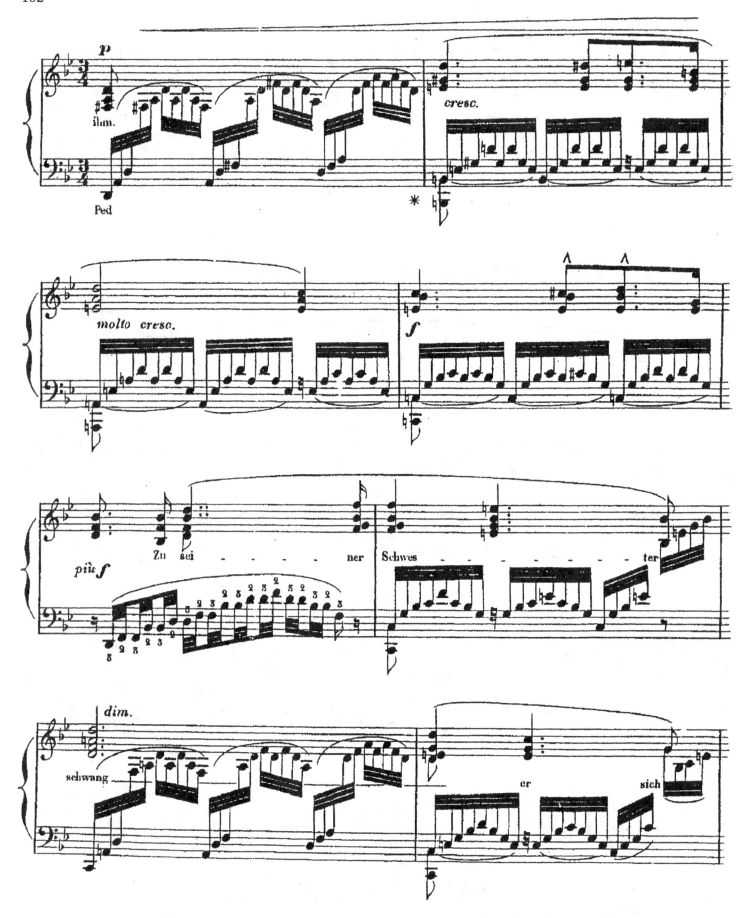

Fine.

Invitation to the Dance

Concert arrangement by Carl Tausig

KARL MARIA VON WEBER

Leipzig: C.F. Peters, ca. 1900

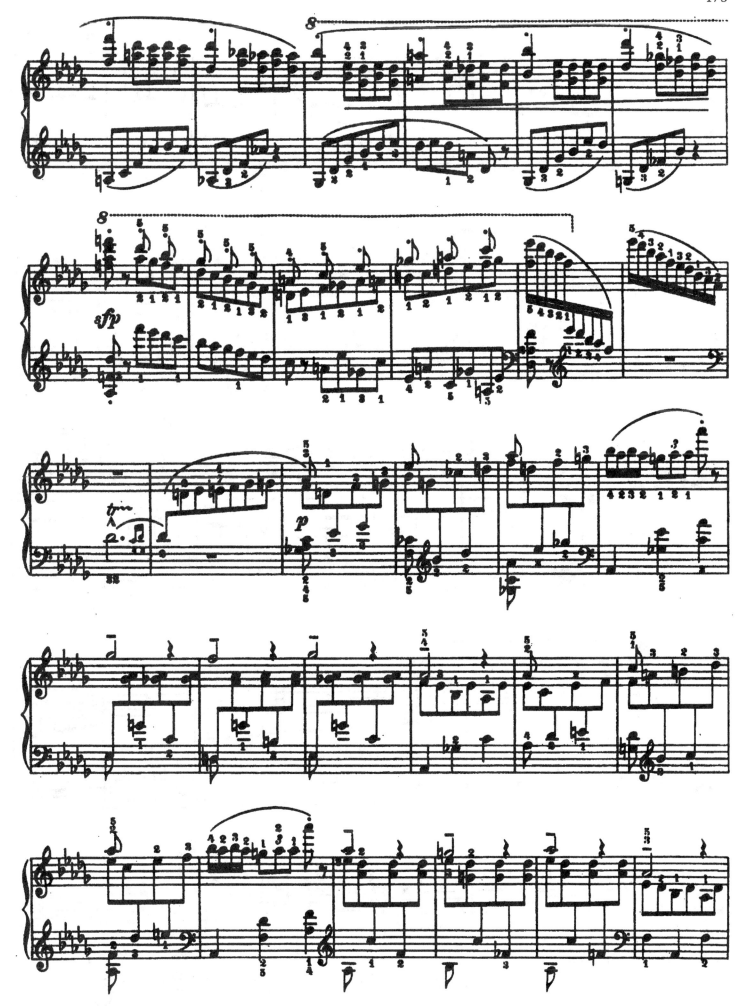

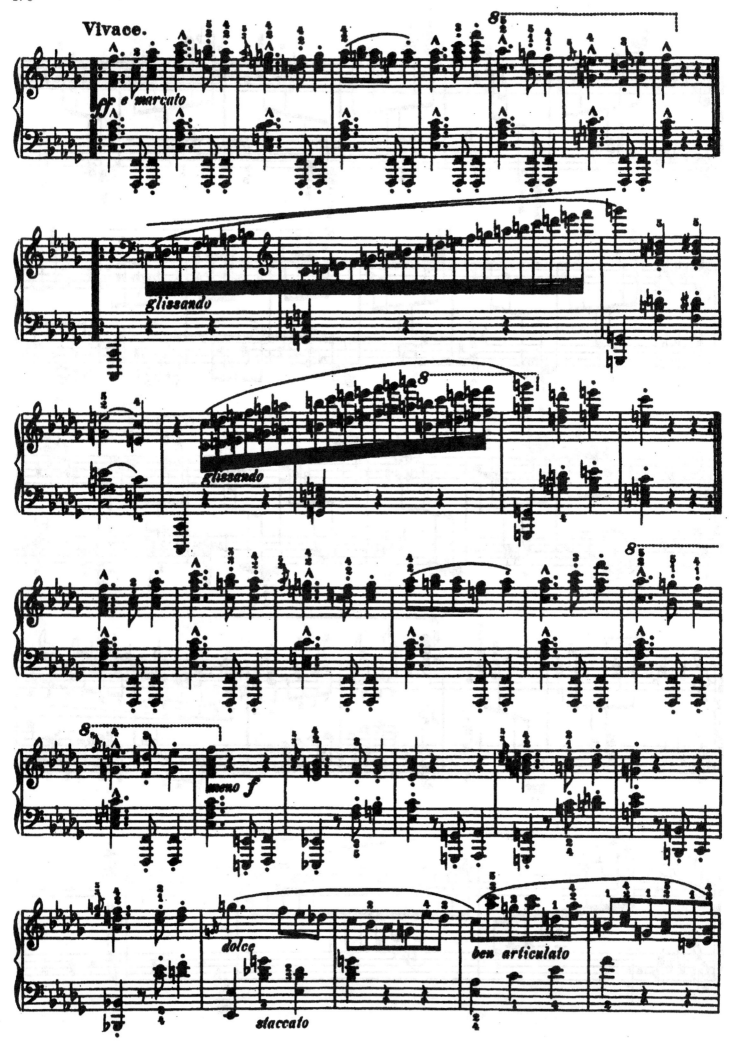